This book is dedicated to all of the
women who felt silenced in their own stories.
To truth telling, growth and healing.

Editor: Sarah Henning
Book Design: Jamal Gamby

Letters to Lola.

erin brown

I don't want to write this. I want to do what feels easy, to put all of this away somewhere in myself and never speak of it again. Some of the details of my life are dark and depressing. I want to believe I can keep my own daughter from those things by omission. But I don't believe in that. I believe what we don't heal we pass on. In ways we can see and ways we don't even realize. I believe that even my drive to silently endure, to pack away, to never look back, was learned from generations of women in my family doing the same.

When I can't see straight, I ask myself, "What would I want for Lola?" Because I know my highest, best self rises to answer that question. What I want for her is to not experience shame as a primary emotion. To know that expressing herself and sharing her experience is always okay. I want her not to wonder about her mother's life, to make easy connections between who I am and was and who she is. I want the same for myself.

So I will write it all down. The dark places I feel inclined to hide. Because I know in my bones it is the path to healing. For all of us.

Dear daughter.

You are still a little girl as I write this. It's hard to believe that one day I will have to let go of this image. Your tiny hands. The constant snuggles. The way you still burrow yourself into me. Your contagious giggle and always smiling nature. I honestly hope to be cool. Not the "cool mom" who buys underage kids alcohol and treats her kids like friends. I want to be the mom you can always talk to. I want to be open to continue to communicate about everything that is happening in your life. I want to protect you but know how limiting that notion is for both of us. I know that it is often from our greatest challenges comes our most profound growth. So instead I hope to guide you, always with highest of intentions.

I have to admit I'm scared. Growing up as a girl was all tutus and pink and fun until puberty. That's when everything got complicated and I didn't have anyone to talk to. I suddenly felt like the enemy. I was taught I was responsible for not only my actions, but for the reactions of men and boys to my existence. My body was changing and so was I. Suddenly getting along with other girls was a whole new world to navigate. And all that on top of just sussing out who I was going to be. What kind of woman would I become?

I worry that you will have these same struggles. Despite all the work I've done. Am doing. I'm fighting, sweet angel. A lot of us are. There are big changes I'd like to see in the world. I've been working as fast as I can to do my part at chipping away at the culturally imposed limitations I faced. That you might have a different world to walk through. But even if I could wave a wand and change these things, life is still going to bring you knocks.

I hope to hold your hand. I would be honored to always be your safe place to land, while you figure out how to find that centering point in yourself. I hope I can be ready to face your changes as they come, and not allow my difficulties in letting go of my little girl stand in the way.

I have no idea what your future holds or mine. There are a lot of things I want you to know. About me. About life. About all the hurting and all the rejoicing. There is so much you will have to learn on your own. I hope to be a guidepost. And if for any reason I cannot be there for you, sweet angel, I wanted to write it all down. At least the highlights.

I love you more than anything.

Mom

On what girls can do.

Girls can do any damn thing they please. The choices available to you are historically significant. The spaces open to you are more vast than ever before. And yet there are still all these unspoken rules we are supposed to follow.

Our appearance is policed, our "tone" unjustly criticised before our words, our "family roles" at times considered a liability.

I'm working at chipping away at all of those expectations and limiting forces. But the best thing you can do is follow your heart wherever it leads you. Question anything that is in your way. Speak right to it. Ask it to move or move it yourself.

We may not be where I want us to be, but baby girl we can be. Girls can do anything they want to. You are a force of nature, when something is in the way, act like it. Mama's got your back.

On self-talk.

I remember being bullied growing up. I was called names. Entire groups of kids would get in on it. I experienced groups of girls deciding I would be the target of "we're not talking to you and we aren't telling you why." I have been "oinked" at, laughed at, mocked, called terrible names. I can recall nearly every insult I've ever been called. None of that was easy to deal with.

But the toughest bully I have ever had to face was the one in my own head.

It wasn't others' words that caused me such struggle, but when their words became the ones I would repeat in my own head. When I would stare in the mirror and pick myself apart. I was the only one there, but the bullying continued. Because it was me. It wasn't their assessments that hurt me, it was my agreement with them.

I attached every unkind word that had ever been said to me to myself. I repeated them over and over. Whenever I perceived a flaw or failure, I would pull from my list of historic insults and rattle them off again.

All of this time I thought I was having a "natural reaction to being me," that anyone who looked like me or was given my set of weaknesses would clearly feel the same way. It didn't occur to me that it was me who was doing the most damage. That what I repeated to myself become the set of limitations by which I lived. That the bully had become me.

It took me a long time to come back from there. Starting with tiny shifts in mantras. Neutral at first as a baby step to positive. It was a purposeful and deliberate process to find a voice in me that liked who I was. And it's one that I still struggle to find when taking a hard knock.

Now, I often use you as my compass. If I'm beginning to get down on myself, to say things to myself I would never say to another, I ask myself what I would want you to say to yourself in this moment. Because I know that what I want from you always comes from the purest love, and that is the same love I aspire to give myself. I aim to give myself what I want for you because we deserve our own love.

Perhaps such a compass can work for you too. Thinking of someone you love, and how you would hope they would buoy themselves in a lapse in self-esteem. Talk to yourself the way you would a friend. Offer encouragement instead of disrespect or insults. The world doesn't always give us it's best. Some lessons come from venom and most poison is in words.

Speaking kindly to yourself doesn't mean complacency, it doesn't mean you think you're better than everyone, it isn't an inflated sense of self. It's an ongoing relationship with you that begins in love and not shame. It's respecting yourself enough to give you your own best. You deserve that.

On coping.

I happen to think all feelings are important. That the pursuit of happiness alone leaves a lot to be desired as bliss comes not just from those beautiful transcendental moments life offers us but from understanding its juxtaposition. While I believe that following what makes your heart sing is an important and valuable way to live, it's unreasonable to believe you are failing when experiencing anything but joy.

Life offers us pain, elation, grief, and sadness (just to name a few) and each of them is its own medicine. Each unlocks a piece of us that wasn't there before. Shows us to a better version of ourselves if we allow it. Cracks open our beliefs, most fundamentally of ourselves, and gives room for us to become.

That doesn't make them easy. Even happiness requires a level of acceptance and presence that can at times be hard to come by.

Coping, for me, looks a lot of different ways. I try to identify my feelings without judging them. Judging myself for my feelings just adds weight and blurs my vision to whatever it is I'm facing. And then ask myself, "What do I need?"

Many of us have forgotten to do this or simply never learned. That we are emotional creatures who deserve our own care and attention. It was only having you that caused me to wake up to this, to be the kind of role model I wanted you to have. When I would no longer use unhealthy numbing mechanisms but actually face myself. My, I have grown.

My coping skills have evolved over time and continue to as I do. Everything evolves. It's best to let it.

Today when I check in with myself to see how I am, I ask myself how I am feeling and what I'd like to do with it. I have learned to befriend my sadness through cleaning, yard work and other quantitative tasks. I listen to sad music, cry and keep my hands busy. I think perhaps the idea that

I'm being productive and sad at once is what is appealing. I can step back after it has "moved" and feel anew. There is also something to clearing your physical space when your head needs it.

When I'm angry I've found letting it out through more aggressive exercise or even just shouting feels good. Singing aggressive songs at the top of my lungs, running sprints, moving quickly seems to let the anger breathe fire instead of incinerate my belly.

When I'm lost I like to write it out. Without judgement or a plan, just let all the words fall freely onto the paper. And when I'm happy I do my best to just savor. Put the phone down. Stop looking anywhere but just right here, right now.

Emotions are meant to come and go. None of them are a residence. Resisting them or attempting to shove them down someplace only gives them space to fester, grow or show up in another kind of pain.

Acknowledging them allows them to move freely. To serve their purpose and go. Coping with them is not about running in the other direction, but marching straight through. Your ways may look completely different than mine, but it is worth seeking. "What do I need?" Is a powerful question many of us have forgotten to ask. I hope you never forget.

On body image.

I want to apologize for the messages from all around that tell you something is wrong with your body. I have to acknowledge the pressure to be ideal. The kind of "ideal" that changes by decade, region, subculture and just who you ask. The kind of ideal that changes so often and always asks that you be more of something and less yourself. That values women in parts and pieces, objects to be admired, reducing our whole personship to "pretty" or failing to be it.

I struggled with this hard. Starting when I was four. I quit ballet because I was certain I was too fat to be there. It was the first of so many things I would quit or not try because I thought my body was somehow wrong and thus I was undeserving.

You saved me from this. When I found out you were coming I knew I had to change forever. That I needed to raise you to love and respect your body as the home you have to live your life in. I knew that in order to do that I had to let go of all the self-hate I had been carrying around.

What I discovered on the other side of constantly belittling myself is that almost every woman and girl I've ever known has a laundry list of things she doesn't like about her body. Thoughts that often live at the forefront of her mind. Most women are constantly aiming for weight loss regardless of their size. As refreshing as it was to jump off that hamster wheel, it was equally startling to be able to really look at it. To see that this phenomenon of self-hatred was not something I was in alone. It was a race we were all running, and all secretly believing we were losing. Now I watch without participating as women find new ways to constantly apologize for themselves, pick themselves apart, and believe that they cannot be who they are meant to be until their appearance somehow changes.

Hopefully this all shifts and your experience will be so different from mine. Hopefully your friends will get together and talk about something other than losing another 10 pounds. But in case things remain the same, I want you to know that there is no size, shape, weight or aesthetic that guarantees happiness. None of those variables make you more or less worthy of love. There is no magic point when the criticism from others or yourself stops. Unless you decide you are enough.

As long as our culture believes that women are mostly here to be looked at, there will be people who pick you apart. Who don't like the way you dress, the way you look, certain parts of your body. At one point in my life I lost 100 pounds. I thought I'd "won." I had finally "fixed" the thing that I believed was so clearly wrong with me. I was completely shocked to find that behind that door was a longer list of new ways I was failing at beauty. It never ends. You have the power to decide you are enough. You have the power to decide your home will not be subject to society's limitations. You are powerful.

It's not easy. But there isn't any other way out. Your body is your home. It is your home to take care of. It is the home that sustains you. Your body's appearance doesn't owe anyone anything. You are not here to be decoration for others' approval.

I'll give it to you straight. The bottom line is women are taught early and often that before they can be worthy of anything else they must first be beautiful—"ideal" looking. The big, nasty trick of it is that there is no way to get there. So we are taught to obsess and sometimes hurt ourselves to attain something ambiguous and always changing. We learn to criticize ourselves and others in the process.

I hope you will join me in stepping out of that mess. I hope you will also find that the pursuit of pretty, especially on such impossible terms, is not what makes you valuable.

I hope that you will do your best to live in alignment with your own values and not those dictated to you. And I hope you can skip some of the heartache I endured while convinced I wasn't enough. You are so very much enough. I'm tired of this. It's exhausting and distracts from just about anything else we could be doing with our time and energy. You are worth so much more.

I hope you live like it.

On being "a bitch."

It wasn't until my thirties that I started asking the question, "What is a bitch?"

I had been called that name so many times, I knew it was something I should avoid. I knew it usually followed my saying something I meant like I meant it. Which unfortunately lead to decades of never saying what I meant for fear of being mislabeled, misunderstood. Other words for "bitch" seem to be "abrasive," sometimes "shrill," or even "aggressive." But sometimes a bitch just means "nasty?" It's so confusing.

I was talking to a friend who was interested in working for a company that was lead by a woman. She was somewhat of a pioneer in this field and positions at her company were hard to come by. As evidenced by the length of time people stayed and personal internal accounts, she was wonderful to work for. And yet she was "known for being a bitch."

This was the first time I ever thought to ask, "What does that mean?" Specifically, "Can you point to the same behaviors in a man and help me understand?" Silence. I started asking around, "What is a bitch? What it the male equivalent of this term?" No one knew.

This was fascinating to me. I had long oscillated from owning it (that's right, I AM a bitch) and completely avoiding it (which sounds like silence and feels like the weight of all your important words crushing your chest as you bury them). And yet no one could tell me what it even was.

The ways to be labeled as such range so dramatically from "actual horrific acts" to "speaking up in a meeting" and even "running a successful business." I have most frequently been called a bitch for speaking up in the name of things I care deeply about, turning down sexual advances made crudely by strangers in public, and simply not smiling.

The good news is this: if no one can tell you what in the world a word means, there is absolutely no reason to fear it. There is no perfect way to avoid it, but there is no perfect reason to either. So carry on, sweet daughter. Say what you mean like you mean it. Including "no."

Someone will likely call you a "bitch," and you can carry the hell on. They don't know what they mean anyway.

On partying, drugs and alcohol.

"I'm probably going to die here." I'm not proud to tell you I have thought that to myself on more than a few drug-induced occasions. Mostly as a young teen. It's truly terrifying to look around the kind of apartment that hosts young people using drugs and believe this is where it ends for you. That is a kind of bleakness I hope you never know.

How I ended up there was a mix of bad choices, struggles I didn't know how to cope with and a burning desire to fit in. It was a way I tried to check out of my life and pretend I was "cool." But I always felt like an imposter. Whatever I was running from only raced faster through my head instead of slowing down. Drugs took more from me than they ever gave me, and I was one of the lucky ones who could easily climb back out. Some people never do.

Here I'm lumping them all together (hard drugs, soft drugs, alcohol) though the individual results and consequences of each are worth weighing alone.

I don't want to just tell you "drugs are bad, don't do them." Because I don't think that speaks to the entire reality of it. There are a lot of drugs that look like a whole lot of fun. But there are reasons to stay away from them anyway, and I want to be honest about what those are to me.

They are illegal. Most drugs are illegal. Which makes for a lot of possible repercussions. One is obvious, you could get caught and be in trouble with the law. That's actually the lesser of my concerns. The bigger concern for me is that illegal drugs are not regulated. Which means you may not be getting what you expect. There are plenty of drug dealers who cut street drugs with household items to yield more profit. In many cases to the detriment of the user—physically, mentally, financially.

To get illegal drugs (or alcohol before you are of legal age) you have to interact with the kind of people who give drugs to kids. I don't mean to underestimate your intelligence or maturity when I say that. But to a grown up, anyone who isn't at least 18 should be seen as a kid. When I think back about the kind of grown-ups who were around when I was acquiring drugs, I'm often surprised I didn't suffer more abuse.

It's scary to be out of control. One too many of anything can be a scary place to be. Even the most "seasoned" user of anything can misstep and find themselves not at the helm. It's frightening to realize you no longer feel in control of yourself. Things get blurry and confusing. You can't leave even if you wanted to. Your body is somehow moving and yet you don't feel like you are the one directing it. It can be terribly frightening.

Sometimes you don't come back. This is rare, honestly. But in my years working in the psych ward, few things were sadder to me than the young people who came in having used a drug once who would never be the same. It triggered something awful. Usually drugs involving formaldehyde. Sometimes drugs cut with household items that can result in death. I hate to be an alarmist, because this is rarely the case. But it's possible and I want you to know all the things.

Addiction changes everything. Some drugs take hold of the user immediatelyand some are addictions are harder to identify. I had a boyfriend in college who drank at a level that concerned me. I mentioned this to one of our mutual friends and was immediately brushed off. "He just likes to party." His response to my concern was much the same. He went on to struggle for many years. It's hard to tell when you are young and have but few responsibilities who is having fun and who is spiraling downward. I have seen addiction tear families apart and change everything about what you can expect from a person. Some people can use addictive drugs recreationally and some cannot.

It might be fun. I can't tell you all of the above and not be honest and tell you I've had some serious fun using drugs. Shots of tequila made for some crazy nights of dancing and a joint sometimes brought a silly conversation with friends to a gut-busting level of euphoria.

It's a lot to weigh. I hope that if you ever have any questions about drugs that you will ask. I will always make sure to find you accurate information about any choices you might make with your body. More than anything I want you to be safe. And my main concern is that drugs present a health and safety risk.

I realize I sound like a junior high health teacher I wouldn't have listened to.

So I'll end with this: I want you to have every delicious experience you desire. If I could cherry-pick these for you, your experiences would only involve trustworthy friends and safe places to be, sober rides home and people who always make sure you get there. And mostly, sweet girl, I hope you see that life offers you so much variety of experience and feeling that you don't feel like you have to turn it up, tune it out or fade away.

On dating.

*See "Sex", "Break-ups", "Marriage". It's all there.

On sex.

The words I often come back to came from a sexologist I once knew. He used to speak to a group I was a part of growing up and he always opened with this, "I'm not here to tell you what your boundaries are. But whether you only hold hands until you are married or you choose to 'go all the way,' all of your shared experiences should be really, really, really good."

Sex isn't necessarily love. It doesn't necessarily create love. It isn't always even intimacy. And it can be all of those things. Heighten existing feelings, be a ridiculously good time. But all it inherently is, is moving parts.

Not just as your mother, but as a woman who respects your autonomy, I hope that you wait to have sex until you feel ready. I hope that this readiness comes later rather than sooner, and is aligned with your own values about how you choose to share your body. Because in ways I will now struggle to articulate, it does change things. It's irreversible.

It changes your relationship to the person you choose to share it with. You become forever linked in an intimate way. For many people, especially with the person with whom they share their first experience.

My opinion, for your consideration: I don't believe sex is a casual thing. Which is not to say that all sex must be shared between people who are deeply in love, but rather that it's worth being thoughtful about. The risk involved in terms of swapping fluids is worth consideration. The potential to create a new life is worth thinking about. Regardless of how, with what terms and with whom you decide to share your body, you are sacred. No choices you make here add to that or take it away.

You deserve to explore your body and your sexuality on terms that feel good to you. I don't hope to tell you what those terms should be, but I hope they never stray from the knowing of how absolutely valuable you are. I hope to be supportive no matter what those choices look like for you.

Now for some useful guidelines. I gave these to my little sister once upon a time. Again; only for your consideration.

24 hours' notice

You can always decide to have sex with someone tomorrow. You can't take back what you do today. It's not a terrible idea to give the notion of sharing your body with another at least 24 hours of thought.

Open communication

Regardless of the boundaries of a relationship, ideally you are with a person with whom you are able to have difficult conversations. About birth control, sexual history, the nature of your relationship. I know none of those things sound "sexy" but open communication is oftentimes more intimate than sex. And avoiding those topics up front does not always mean you get to avoid them forever, depending on the possible outcomes of your interaction.

Mutual consent

Both parties should provide on-going enthusiastic consent to all actions. I know I said "for your consideration," but this one is big. It's always okay to change your mind. At any point, either person can back out. Mutual consent is the difference between "that was a great experience" and even just "FUN!" and scars that live on indefinitely, sometimes forever.

Safety precautions

A potentially uncomfortable conversation about condoms is a lot less challenging than an uncomfortable conversation about herpes or an accidental pregnancy.

I didn't always make the best decisions about my own sex life. Mostly because of insecurities, wanting someone to like me, and an on-going belief that perhaps this was all I had to offer. I have consented to acts I wasn't comfortable with and didn't want to participate in for many reasons that weren't my own desires.

It really wasn't until recent years that I came to think of sex as something that was for me at all, and not just something given away, allowed or used. I hope that isn't the case for you.

I have found sex to be exciting, awkward, strange, fun and exhilarating. Sometimes all of that at once. It took me a long time to understand what felt good to me and what I liked. To engage in sex, not just for the other person, but for my own pleasure. Most of that knowing came from exploring myself alone.

Whatever choices you make, I hope you know you can talk to me. I would never be disappointed in you. These things are complicated, and even with best laid plans can leave behind more emotionally charged feelings than expected. If it's not me you talk to, I hope you go to your aunt or someone you trust. You don't have to navigate this alone. It doesn't have to come with shame even if you feel you misstep.

I hope you have the best time ever exploring yourself. I hope everything you choose for yourself is "really, really, really good."

On masturbation.

I'm aware this may be a space in which you don't want to hear your mother's stories. So I'll make this short and to the point. Your body is your own. This is a great way to get to know it, relieve stress and discover what you like. All worthwhile endeavors.

On being sensitive.

If your current personality is in any way indicative of the woman you are to become, you, my darling, are a sensitive being. I recognize this so clearly in you as it is something we share. You feel what others are feeling, you experience joy and heartache for yourself and others profoundly. You are aware of your emotional state and that of others.

This, sweet girl, is a wonderful gift. But it is also one that can be difficult to navigate. Our greatest weakness is our strength mismanaged. Being sensitive can lend itself to poor boundaries with others. It can lead to wanting to "rescue" everyone around you all the time. It can be overwhelming to be in groups or around the hurting.

The first thing I want you to know is that being sensitive is absolutely a strength. It is a strength that I believe is often undermined or belittled because it is thought of as being "feminine." But regardless of the gender of the sensitive person, this is a strength. And one I'm not sure can be taught. To understand and know intimately your own emotional body and be able to understand those around you—this is the embodiment of strength.

I also want you to know that you cannot carry others' experiences for them. By that I mean, consciously or un-consciously attempting to carry the load of someone else's burdens, does not lessen their load. All it does is add to your own. I believe that we can only carry what is ours. That our lives give us our own hand of emotional difficulties, and we alone carry them, sort through them, face them or attempt to bury them. No one can take them from us but us. Try, sweet girl, to be the kind of friend who listens without being overwhelmed. Who can offer support without offering your whole self. We have to hold space enough for others to carry their own experience. We cannot take it from them.

I hope that you notice the depth of your joy as much as your sorrow. It can be easy to focus on all that is wrong. Especially when you feel as deeply as you do. But if we only see what is heavy, we miss a whole beautiful part of life. We miss the light. I hope that as you learn to navigate your emotional body, that you relish in your light as well. Know that the same part of you that recognizes the depth of sadness can roll around in the breadth of happiness as well. I'm not suggesting you don't experience your challenges, but rather that you allow yourself to deeply experience your joys as well. Neither should swallow you whole.

Letters to Lola

On health.

- Use sunscreen.

- Stay hydrated.

- Move purposefully regularly.

- Feed yourself well.

- Get plenty of sleep.

- Laugh.

- Be quiet sometimes.

- Feel your feelings.

- Take walks in the sunshine.

Those are the basics. So many health practices are sold to us with shame. Framed as the pursuit of pretty. Wrapped up in "shoulds" or laughed off as impractical.

But it doesn't have to be so complicated. Take basic care of yourself. Do your best. Your body will thank you and your life will be more manageable.

On beauty.

I have always wanted to be beautiful. And, likewise, never thought that I was. I had moments. A new outfit or haircut had me momentarily feeling proud of my appearance. But it always felt like it was immediately taken away by someone else. By their being more beautiful, or commenting that I wasn't or perhaps just looking at me in a way I was certain meant they thought I was ugly. It became an obsession and one that didn't serve me well. For many, many years.

One of the things adults were always saying to me was, "beauty is on the inside." And, daughter, that is certainly true. However that sentiment never made me feel any better about myself. It felt synonymous with ugliness. Still, I tried that mantra on anyway.

It wasn't until I had you that I came to understand beauty for myself. You were the most beautiful thing I had ever seen. I stared at you for hours, marveling at every feature. This had nothing to do with how you "measured up" to other babies. I wasn't lining you up with babies in commercials or at library storytime to determine you were the "best." You were the best and most beautiful because I loved you ferociously.

I didn't take you in parts to criticize—I simply drank in your image in awe.

It was then that I realized that beauty has nothing to do with standards, comparison or even cultural ideals. It's truly subjective. And what a wonderful thing.

We seek beautiful things. Some people travel all over the world to look at beautiful art or landscapes. Just to admire them. We fill our spaces with things we think are beautiful, that make us happy. And each curated space is unique to the person behind it. Why then would we strive either to be the same or to end the expansiveness of that lens in our mirrors?

Like so many things, this will be something for you to determine for yourself. What is beauty? Is it important to you? How important and why? All of those questions will require your own thoughtful conclusions. And those can and often do change.

Today your mother celebrates beauty, sees it everywhere. Certainly in you. And also certainly in me. It isn't a contest, it isn't a race. There are no winners and losers. It's a deep appreciation for diversity and expression. It is in the mountains, in a paint brush, in darkness, and in my reflection. I hope whatever conclusion you come to brings you as much peace.

On friendship.

Relationships can be the grounding force in an otherwise chaotic time and they can be wrought with heartache. I have found most of mine to be some of each. But the latter should never become your norm.

I once had a group of friends with whom I did everything. We talked about everything, were always at one another's houses, were the first to know about anything new in each other's lives. We were a crew.

We were also very unhealthy. I wasn't able to see this until I went on a family vacation and for the first time was physically removed from my friends. My parents took us to Wyoming where we would ride horses and stay in cabins and enjoy the view. I was miserable. Hours in the car with my little sister, certain my parents were trying to torture me. In spite of this being one of very few vacations we took as a family, I couldn't be convinced it was fun.

In the separation, my world view opened wide up. I had been so caught up in my friendships and our "goings on" that I couldn't see anything objectively. My world had become very small. Leaving that behind meant interacting with other people. For the first time in ages I was looking up at the sky. I was having independent thoughts I wasn't running past the same few people before deciding what to think.

I realized that not only was the group I was spending all of my time with headed down a dangerous path, but they weren't good friends to me. They made fun of me a lot. I was so wrapped up in this crew I couldn't see that I always felt worse about who I was after being with them. I saw the path they were taking was not one I wanted for myself and had to step aside.

I came back from that summer vacation feeling more like myself than ever before. But transitioning from being a "member of the group" to an outsider was rough. My old friends gave me a hard time about how I "never hang out anymore." There were comments about me thinking "I was too good for them." It made them uncomfortable. It was tough. But it was right for me.

Even though I would go on to later be in a sorority and run in close circles of girlfriends, it was the last time I allowed my identification to be up to a group. Part of this, I think, is a natural part of growing up—beginning to be clear about your own values instead of vetting them by others at all times. But there's a bigger nugget here that I would continue to use in my adult years.

All relationships are not healthy. Even if they are long. Even if they involve love. Even when everyone has good intentions.

Jim Rohn said, "You are the average of the five people you spend the most time with." I'm a good arguer—I could argue that quote either way. But it does draw an important conclusion about influence. Who we are with matters. It affects not only the choices we make but who we become.

Baby girl, I hope you never get caught up in a group of friends that isn't good for you. But I hope that you know that no matter where you end up and with whom, you can always change course. I don't know who I would be today if I had stayed there. My gut told me I had to go, I hope you learn to listen to your own gut.

Friendships should be good for your soul. Great friendships challenge us to be better versions of ourselves. And sometimes we have to stop and evaluate in ANY relationship, if it's best for us to stay there.

Loving someone doesn't always mean you stay, not when it means you can't love yourself there.

On what everyone else is doing.

Life is not a race, sweet girl. But you wouldn't know it to look around you. Everything from weight loss to degree collecting looks like a battle to the finish line. In this way, it is so easy to feel like a failure. With so many roads to choose from, you cannot go every way simultaneously. You have instead to choose paths as wisely as you can in the moment and be open to choosing a new direction when your inner wisdom tugs at a new way.

This is enough work. It's enough to grapple with. It's enough to keep you up at night, sometimes in excitement and sometimes in fear. As each new "yes" is also a "no" to something else. If you look up from your navel gazing and see "what everyone else is doing," you will inevitably be even more confused. You will perhaps experience envy and pity and relief and overwhelming anxiety that you are ahead or behind or just certainly in the wrong place.

I dropped out of college. I dropped out two classes short of a degree. Two classes that didn't come easily and gave me much anxiety. The kind that makes you sweat in bed at night but not the kind that leads to action. For many years I skirted around this. At first I would say "I haven't finished yet." But as time wore on I began telling people "I studied social work in college" as a way to express that I had higher education without admitting I didn't complete my degree. I worried about who would find out and what they would think of me. Perhaps they will all think I'm a fraud. A failure.

Two things worth mention here.

> 1) I literally have no idea who "all these people" were I knew were going to judge me. I just felt paralyzed by the thought of them.

2) I would never judge someone else in the ways I have always feared I would be judged.

Statistics is one of the classes that stumped me. I attempted it twice and failed each time. Looking at my homework felt like trying to read a novel in a language I'd never even heard of. I felt certain that this was evidence of my own stupidity. For almost 10 years I wished someone would take the burden from me—I wanted someone to come along and offer to take it for me. I told myself I would do the same for someone else, taking an entry level sociology class just to finally get them off the hook.

I was resentful of people with degrees. I would tell myself I was just as smart as them. That this was all so very unfair.

Eventually I stopped focusing on what I didn't have and who I didn't think I was, and started working on what I felt inspired by. I started writing, I began the work I do now. And, over time, I became less afraid of what I wasn't, or how I measured up to others. Because I'd found a more comfortable home in my own life and my own choices.

Then my Statistics Angel walked into my life. I met her via email, making arrangements to be her roommate at a conference we would both attend. She seemed pretty rad and I was excited to make a new friend. And then I googled her.

Statistics Angel had a doctorate degree in statistics from Harvard. My jaw dropped. I felt a sea of envious emotions and almost as immediately, a sense of calm. I knew this was significant.

We became the kind of fast friends that are truly a gift in adult life. We shared stories, insecurities, tears. On the first day I told her "I dropped out of college." Perhaps I was in a rush to tell her that, to get my baggage out of the way. But

I heard myself use those words for the first time and it wasn't scary at all. It was true. And it didn't tell the whole story of me. Just like her degrees didn't tell the whole story of her. Just like any one set of knowing about a person cannot begin to tell you all of the brutal and honest and wonderful truths that lie beneath the surface.

At the end of the weekend she offered to take the class for me. It was as though the thought just popped in her head and out of her mouth at once. Here was what I wanted. Not just someone to unburden me, but the opportunity to finally measure up in this way. With no contemplation and complete certainty, I told her through tears that I loved her so much for offering and that I didn't need her help. I had dropped out of college.

This is not a story about degrees. It's a story about choices. I know my friend made a lot of sacrifices on her path. I did too. We both missed out on countless things because of the roads we chose to follow. Owning my own choice allowed me to admire hers without comparison. Owning my choice allowed me to honor all of the paths I'd chosen and what gifts had come from them.

I believe quite honestly that you can do and be and become whatever you can imagine. But everything comes with a cost. That is true for everyone and every choice. It's hard not to measure your perceived weaknesses up to someone else's strengths. To look up from your life and wonder if perhaps you should have picked the way someone else has.

You can always change. You can always turn around. You can always pick a new course. But you can never, ever win all the races. You have to choose which ones to run, honor your own pace, and allow others the space to do the same.

On consent.

I've been pacing to avoid this topic. I have sat down to write this over and over again and found a million other things to do instead. As a result of needing to write this chapter I have cleaned out my email inbox to zero more than once, a completely miraculous feat. But I don't want to leave out the parts that matter most. This is one of those.

When I was 13 years old I consented to kiss a boy. When I was 13 years old I consented to kiss a boy who then raped me. He held me down and I eventually gave up the fight. I laid motionless. An event that would change my life forever. I thought it was my fault. I thought I had caused it. I have thought about that night countless times. Rethinking every moment, what I wore, how I behaved, how I could have caused this.

I grew up in a culture that taught me to do that—to believe that violence against me is a result of my existence. My fault. I never thought to ask myself, "Why did he feel entitled to attack me?" "Why didn't he stop when I said, 'no'?"

I didn't get help largely because I felt responsible and silenced. And though as an adult I have stood before hundreds if not thousands of people and told my story aloud, telling it to you breaks my heart all over again. I want to somehow save you from the dark places I've been. But the trouble is that all of me shows up to parent you. Your mother is a whole person, with a rich history that in my case includes abuse.

I've been working on unwinding the damage for almost two decades now. Layer upon layer of hurt so nuanced and vague yet real and trying, exposing itself to me as I go. I've learned to speak about it, to end my shame, to address my anger, to fight. I still struggle to feel safe sometimes. It has impacted every romantic relationship since.

I want better for you, and I so feverishly want to protect you from such an experience. Though there isn't any one thing I can do to ensure that. But I will tell you this.

Your body is yours and yours alone. You have the absolute right at any moment to determine its experience. You can change your mind. You can say yes and no exactly as you mean it. You have the right to always be the one who decides what is next for your own body. There is no action on your part that justifies violence in another. Your choices with your body may be difficult to make. Always shoot for a big "yes" over a maybe. You don't owe anyone your body, and no one gets to take your autonomy from you.

It is yours.
It is yours.
It is yours.

And I will support you unwaveringly, always. But consent is not just about abuse or legal ramifications, it's also about ensuring a positive experience. It should be fun. Any way you choose to share yourself with another should be full of "yes!" Each person involved has a right to say what they want and those actions have to be agreed on. Not just to avoid trauma but to ensure a good time.

Consent doesn't look like motionless defeat. It's both parties actively involved in what is happening. Expressing satisfaction. It's "YES!" Not just the absence of loud no's and dramatic fight.

I worry when we teach that sex is a conquest, we miss that it is a shared experience. One that deserves mutual clear intentions, everyone's pleasure in mind and thoughtful communication.

So your autonomy matters. Every single time you choose to share your body with another, it deserves to be with a big "yes!" with someone who you trust to respect if your yes becomes a no. These decisions are difficult for everyone, but they always lie squarely with you.

Your body.
Your autonomy.
Your self-governance.

Yours.

On boundaries.

"No" is a complete sentence. It's one with which a lot of us struggle. We want to give reasons, to bury the "no" in a bunch of smaller "yeses." To somehow justify what often really boils down to "I don't want to" or "this is not my priority." Which are completely okay things to say.

I found my "no" at 17. Much, much later than I'd have liked. A boy I'd once dated for a few weeks in junior high who broke up with me because I didn't "put out" called me out of the blue. He was cute and paying attention to me so my then insecure self was very excited. Until he started talking.

After a few short minutes of flirting and catching up he proposed the following: because he couldn't "picture us" being a couple or going on dates, he thought we could just secretly have sex. He went on to share that he felt I "owed him" this because he dated me before and already had "put in the time."

I remember this moment so clearly because it was the first time I felt myself plant my feet into a "no." It was a big no. A hell no. A "I can't believe anyone thinks they can talk to me like this and I'm going to fix that right here and now" no.

While this was a gift that came in a bizarre package, it's one I'm still grateful for. All gifts don't come in love, this one came to ground me in my feet and reclaim my fire.

More regular "nos" in my life now involve not volunteering for things I don't want to do. Not going places I don't want to go if invited. Not hanging out with people who I feel badly around. And on and on.

"No" serves both as a clear boundary between yourself and the thing you want no parts of, as well as a big "yes" to time and energy to devote to things you actually want to give time and energy to. I try to keep this in mind when I have to say no and feel badly, that I am in fact leaving lots of space for yeses later.

I only recently learned how amazing it feels to let go of obligation, too. I thought I was obligated to do so many things I didn't want to. It wasn't until I turned that around at myself that I realized what a disservice this was to everyone.

I would never want someone to go out of their way because they felt "obligated" to me. To do me a favor or help in some way while secretly feeling unhappy about it. Now when I find myself feeling obligated when my real answer is "no," I go straight for the no. It's so much less complicated, so much easier, such a weight lifted. It gives me more time, space and energy to people and things that get a clear "yes" from me.

When you were a baby, your protest cries were the best. Full lungs, full-on angry cries. These, as you might imagine, were not fun to listen to. I remember your daddy once saying to me over the sound of your wailing that "this is a girl who has found her no." It was such a beautiful change of perspective for me. You, baby girl, have found your no. Don't ever lose it. It is valuable, it matters and it's yours. Use it everywhere and anywhere you see fit.

On mottos.

A motto is a short phrase to live by. Different mottos have served me at different times in my life. Often they have been others' words that have inspired action in me when I couldn't find my own. Sometimes they were self-deprecating and didn't serve me at all. Either way they are words we come back to, words that frame our understanding of our experience.

I can't wait to hear what inspires you.

I have two mottos that I keep coming back to that might be of service to you. They are simple and effective to me.

The first is "it's fine."

Most of the time I find the things I stress about turn out "fine." They are situations and circumstances that pass. Often quickly when I don't let them derail me. Rather than find all of the possible reasons a stressor "should" take me all the way off course, I skip to "it's fine," because in most cases it will be.

When it's not fine, the second is, "it's perfect."

I have come to trust that whatever isn't easily fixed will serve me in the best way. Perhaps with difficult growth or mustering courage to address hard things. The biggest challenges of my life have always ended up being the perfect lesson, propelling me forward in a way that I didn't know was necessary.

"It's fine," and "it's perfect," have kept me from jumping off into despair. Telling myself terrible stories of who I am or how I have failed, who has hurt me or what is unfair. I have found either or both to always be true and I derive great comfort from that.

On doing what scares you.

There is a distinct difference between danger and something that is as scary it's electrifying. One threatens you and one takes hold of you and won't let go. Lures you in and begs you to try.

When I was younger there were so many things I didn't try because I was scared or certain I couldn't do it. As early as 13 I began writing off potential habits, thinking it was "too late" for me to develop a new skill. I was always afraid I would fall on my face. I was terrified of embarrassment.

So I did nothing.

I feigned apathy to disguise my fear. Not caring about anything seemed much cooler than failing at something. But I longed to have "a thing," something of my own, a hobby or skill to develop. I wanted to breathe new life into me.

I wasted a lot of time that way. And I didn't avoid much embarrassment either. That's just a part of growing up.

In my adult life I have a much different philosophy. I take note of everything that scares me and run toward it. Not danger, rational fears - but those that excite me. I delight at being terrible at new stunts. Laugh my way through the process of being brand new. Certainty of embarrassment has been replaced by taking myself less seriously. I revel in how alive I feel stretching myself in new ways.

At times the things that scare me are easy to decipher. Like finally conquering the rope climb I never nailed in elementary school gym class. Others seem rooted deeper, in baggage and darkness I can't see as clearly. Irrational fears that feel as though they are asking me for some kind of redemption. Saddling up to those has offered me great healing, shifting unmovable parts that have been stuck for too long.

Even the things I am passionate about can feel scary. The possibility of failure seems so big when I fully allow myself to care. Every single time before I set foot on a stage to speak my heart races and my body seems certain I will die. Butterflies surge in my stomach. I have to purposefully make sure I feel connected to my feet. And yet that is the exact place I feel certain I should be. It matters so much to me that the risk of face planting is just worth it.

Do what interests you. Chase what ignites your passion. Try what excites you. You will fall down. You might embarrass yourself. But you might also stumble upon the thing that brings you the most joy. Maybe even some healing. The things that make life magic require you move outside your comfort zone. And remind you you're alive.

On depression.

The earliest I remember having depression symptoms was junior high. I didn't want to go to school. I didn't want to get out of bed. I often just didn't want to do anything at all. High school was more of the same. Warm weather (sunshine + being more active) was always good for me. It wasn't all dark and dreary but college came with more difficulties.

The first couple years of college were great for me academically. I made friends and was for the most part happy. I had serious issues with confidence which I hid well, but I think having success in the classroom and respect of my professors did a lot for the those first years.

Then things changed.

There was a series of academic rejections that knocked my new-found confidence.

There was upsetting news from home.

I was also sick, all the time. Lots of digestive problems. Serious digestive problems that landed me in the ER on IVs more than once a year. I had to call in sick so frequently it started to feel like lies, even if I was actually in the hospital.

And then one day it felt like I'd slipped quick sand and just couldn't stop sinking.

I became apathetic. I slept all day. I didn't care about doing things. I was suddenly unable to envision a future for myself so planning for one didn't seem necessary.

The worst part about depression, for me, is that it feels impossible to explain to anyone.

It looks like laziness.

I felt so desperate to be understood and yet so hopeless that anyone would understand. So I began to internalize feelings of worthlessness, hopelessness, and started thinking, "maybe I am just lazy." I had a lot to do. I didn't want to do any of it. It felt impossible. I felt incapable. I felt like nothing.

At one point I hadn't left my house in so long my roommate conned me into going outside, locked the doors and forced me to go out with her (in my slippers!), she was a damn good friend. I remember a really sweet and well-meaning boyfriend suggesting I workout. He talked about endorphins and it being good for depression. All I could hear is that he was calling me fat.

After having to meet with my advisor because of slipping grades I knew I had to do something. So I went to student health and I got myself a prescription for antidepressants and started seeing a therapist.

Therapy is great. I tend to think everyone can benefit from therapy. But you have to find the right therapist for you. This first round was not the right fit.

The dude wanted to talk to me about his morning routine—I now understand why he started this way, but it wasn't helpful at the time. After much discussion of how he takes his coffee then we would move on to talking about my father.

It felt like he went to school and learned that when women have issues it has something to do with their fathers and that is the only possibility. I assured the guy my relationship with my father was fine, that there was actually a lot of things I wanted to talk about and that wasn't one of them. But the more I insisted that wasn't the issue the more he felt it was. Bottom line; he didn't listen to me and I quit seeing him.

The antidepressants made me different.

On the antidepressants I didn't feel so hopeless but I mostly felt nothing. I didn't feel happy. I felt hollow. I felt how you do when you haven't slept enough in a really long time but you have drunk enough coffee that you can go through the motions. You don't really feel anything, you don't even feel present, but you can now do things.

So I took myself off of them abruptly, and experienced the most incredible crash—physically and emotionally. At this point I was so worn out and I had no idea what to do. I just wanted it fixed. And since the therapist didn't "fix" me and the drugs didn't "fix" me, well what the hell was going to fix me?! I felt like a lost cause. A person who once had so much potential but was now just a shell. Around me it felt like people moved on. I felt stuck.

This is when the anxiety part got worse. I started having somewhat regular anxiety attacks. These basically feel like you are suddenly dying. The worst one I remember happened when I was in the computer lab at school one night and I felt like I couldn't breathe. I ran to the bathroom and put my head between my legs and tried to catch my breath. I felt crazy. My chest hurt. I thought I might pass out. It felt completely surreal. I had no frame of reference for how long it lasted, but I was eventually able to catch my breath, pick myself up off the floor and go back to whatever I was doing. Not a happy college memory.

I know the sentiment from some of my friends at that time is that I "dropped off." I did. But it wasn't some inspired decision to spend less time with friends or go less frequently to class. I was gone from me.

There wasn't some great "ah-ha" moment where everything became awesome again. I spent a lot of time alone. I used that time to work on building myself back up. I moved. I didn't have "unfinished business" where I went to college that I was running from but there was a lot of old baggage it was nice to leave behind. I had less on my plate and what felt like a fresh start.

It wasn't until I started taking care of myself that I was able to feel better for long stretches at a time. It was honestly shocking to me to find how different I felt mentally and emotionally when I began to taking care of me. Moving my body regularly with purpose. Feeding myself thoughtfully with foods to which my body responded well. What I now consider basic self-care was nowhere present in my life and yet I didn't begin to draw a connection between the two things.

Everyone is different. Our bodies respond differently to the different things. We require different measures of care for different ailments. But I have come to believe that for me, keeping my head above water requires more than going through the motions every day. So I offer myself lots of compassion, daily check-ins, and mounds of self-care.

Mental health battles can feel isolating, but should you ever struggle yourself, you are not alone. There are lots of options for help and none of them have to come with shame. I never want you to spend hours, let alone years, feeling like you are drowning. Like no one understands. Should you ever find yourself unstable, there is always support to be had. Life can be hard but it shouldn't feel impossible. There is always help. Even if your first attempts to get it don't stick. Your life is worth showing up for, and sometimes we all need some help to get back there.

On self-care.

I hope I have instilled in you a sense that you deserve your own time, energy and care. I reorganized my whole life when you came in an effort to show you just that. But I can't change the messages from everywhere else.

Women are taught to be martyrs. That we are here only to serve and nurture others. That we should remain last on our own lists of priorities if present at all.

Yet, I've never heard a man utter such a sentiment. To frame items on his own list of priorities for himself as a means to do more for others. "I have to play a few rounds of golf so that I can be a better husband and father" are words I've never heard a man say. Not ever.

You don't stop mattering if you choose to become a mother. You don't stop mattering if you choose to become a wife. You don't have to cease to matter if you choose to be neither of those things.

You matter. You matter. You matter. For your whole life you matter. Regardless of what roles and identities you take on.

It seems like such a simple thing, but it's one that is so full of guilt for so many of us. It's such a revolutionary thought that a woman spend time and energy on her own desires and needs, that we attach words like "selfish" to it. It's not selfish at all. It's self-preservation, it's thriving, it's putting into action the belief that you are valuable. It's survival.

You deserve quiet and loud. Dancing and stillness. Rolling around in the mud or basking in a bath. Whatever it is that fills your soul, you deserve. And you deserve to give that to your own self. Every day.

Self-care is crucial.

This kind of self-sufficiency allows anyone and anything you chose for your life to be additions to greatness instead of measures of rescue. You deserve a big, juicy life. And you can give all of that to yourself. I love you so madly. And I won't be here forever. Please take amazing care of my baby girl. You most certainly deserve that. From yourself. Always.

On the decision to have a baby.

In my short life I have seen a lot of social change here. More women are choosing not to have children, instead deciding to focus on their own lives or careers or relationships. They are choosing autonomy instead of family. There are still stigmas attached to this choice—there are stigmas, sweet girl, attached to about everything.

I'm excited to see this shift. Not because I'm against mothering, but because I am so excited about choices. About women seeing their entire lives as being for their own choosing. This is relatively new.

Having a baby is such a big decision. And it's one you can only make for yourself and with your partner. So here are some things to factor in.

Your life will never be the same. Unlike having a dog you can put in a kennel, your child is your responsibility all the time. Tattoos and childcare are two things I recommend never finding on clearance. It's an investment financially, spiritually, and energetically. One you make for the rest of your life.

You'll never be ready. Planning is great in any endeavor, of course. But if you look at a calendar or a calculator to tell you if you're ready—the answer will almost always be no. There is no way to feel 100 percent prepared. So it's okay if you don't.

This is a huge decision, and one you'll have to make almost entirely yourself. It's worth spending some time thinking about what it is you want for your own life before even approaching this decision with a partner.

Nothing could have prepared me for how you would change my life.

I was 24 and working as a social worker. I rolled into work not feeling great but, as a person who took mediocre care of herself, that was normal for me at the time. A co-worker asked me if I had time to drop her client off at elementary school for her and I obliged. He got in my car and started eating Cheetos and I have never been more repulsed by a smell in my life. It felt like the entire car was full to the brim with Cheeto-flavored dust and I could barely breathe. This was not normal.

I stopped at a local grocery store and picked up a pregnancy test. I found out I was pregnant in the bathroom stall at my job. I called your father who worked nearby and asked if he could take a break. I was scared. Was this right for my life? We had talked about having kids but not right now. How would he react? He welled up a bit, I've only ever seen this from him a few times, and the words he said I will never forget, "This is everything I've ever wanted."

I know many people do this alone. I cannot be more grateful that I have your father to raise you with me. He talks me off the ledge when I'm exhausted, brings me back down to earth when my mind travels a bit too far and loves us both ferociously.

When I was in labor and in so much pain, he kept repeating to me, "Just think about holding our baby." It has been clear to me ever since that this man is my rock.

A lot of having a baby is magical. Those first few days at home together were nothing short of a dream. Becoming a family together. Teamwork. Sleepless nights felt like a gift for us to explore together.

A lot of having a baby is decidedly not magical. Sleepless nights become the challenge that leads to the brink of unravel. The third poopy diaper "blow out" of the day can bring you to your knees. And the helpless feeling of "am I doing this all wrong?" is one I know most parents struggle with.

To be honest, I lost myself in you for awhile. Those first few years I wasn't sure who I was anymore outside of the care-taker of you. "Mommy" became my entire identity which was both hard on my sense of self and on our marriage. You were the beginning, the middle and the end.

I wouldn't take one second of it back. Those years were formative for both of us. Sealed the bond we have today. And yet when your father and I discuss the possibility of having another baby, neither of us can imagine going back there.

As you gained independence, walking, toilet training, eventually going to school, we found our way back to ourselves and one another. Every piece of that journey has been meaningful and dotted with transcendental moments of gratitude.

There is something almost inherently growth inducing about willingly unraveling yourself out of love. I became who I am today because of you.

But while having you is perhaps the best thing I have ever done, I balk at the idea that this is the only way to have a glorious life. That we are somehow obliged to have children or our lives are deemed insignificant or meaningless.

Should you have a baby? That is a great question. It's one I hope you take time to consider. There will be no right or wrong answer, just the one that calls to you. All major life decisions begin in a leap of faith. So I hope you choose your own adventure thoughtfully. My footsteps are here but you don't have to follow them. I'm excited to support you endlessly in whatever direction you leap.

On what you wear.

Oh how I loathe all the messages you are likely to receive about this. Some camps extoll the virtues of modesty, the importance of covering everything up. Some go further to shame girls and women who choose to show skin in any scenario, even believing that it is the cause of abuse. Troubling to me are the messages that say your body is a "distraction" to men, as though they aren't accountable for their own behavior in the face of skin. And others believe this whole conversation is about an awareness of judgement from others, that you should carefully make choices about your appearance so that you "send the right message" about who you are.

My struggle with all of that is that these stipulations are unfairly weighted on women. In the same schools that don't allow tank tops on girls, boys are allowed to run shirtless. Likewise, even as an adult woman, there doesn't seem to be any way I can present myself that comes without judgement.

So what are you to do? Baby girl, these choices will be yours.

Even now I struggle with what to tell you about this. As your father and I speak together about the appropriateness of your shorts, if they cover "enough" to be "outside of the house" clothes—I have to stop to question why this is a concern. I ask myself if we would even have this conversation if you were a boy. I really don't know.

A part of me that is conditioned by misogyny and driven by love, wants to believe that keeping you "covered" is the same as keeping you safe. But I also know that that is not true. I want to tell you to dress in a way that ensures that your ideas will supercede your appearance, that ensures you are heard and not just seen. But no such outfit exists to guarantee that either.

We live in a community that is mostly welcoming of wildness in appearance. Where extremes in hair color, vibrant clothing and tattoos are mostly viewed as colorful. But you don't have to drive more than 20 miles in any direction to find a community where these same attributes come with a whole host of unfair stereotypes.

The only way to navigate this well is with your own compass. You may have to remind me that as you grow. There is no way to dress that keeps you safe or unnoticed. There is no way to dress that ensures you are taken seriously. There is no way to dress that will perfectly articulate who you are or immediately garner respect.

If you find that you enjoy clothing, perhaps as a fun way to communicate who you are or what you love, then enjoy it! If you find that clothing is more utilitarian for you, that it just needs to get you from here to there and make sense for what you will do, then do that. None of these choices alone will define you. Neither will others' judgements about them.

If there was a perfect way to show up in the world as a woman, I would tell you. Instead you have to determine what all of that means to you. It's all messy unless it's confidently yours. I'll always be here to help you navigate, but these decisions will lie squarely with you.

On high school.

High school sucked.

That short sentence sums up my attitude toward the whole thing. I was old enough to have become somewhat grounded in a sense of who I was. Smart enough to find the social politics ridiculous. I felt totally invisible and somewhat thankful for that. I was a complete cynic.

I viewed the whole thing as a necessary evil between myself and the rest of my life. And I could easily justify all of those feelings. They were very much real to me. I still cringe a bit when I think about walking in those hallways again.

And yet, I really feel like I missed out on something.

I can't imagine a world where I would have been homecoming queen or otherwise deemed important by the select few charged with making that distinction. But in my effort to remain under the radar, I did nothing very productive with that time. And after all, it was several years of my life.

I spent time being annoyed at the teachers who played into the social structure, giving special attention to star athletes and cheerleaders. I gave energy to people who were unkind to me. I think I basically rolled my eyes for three full years.

Senior year I had a writing teacher who was one of the best teachers I'd ever had. He was tough. He would literally throw my work back at me. Not if it wasn't the best, but if he could tell I didn't try. He expected our best work on every piece we ever wrote. Pushed us to write far beyond the gimmicky way we had learned to write essays, opening with "Webster's definitions" or rhetorical questions. He made me care. I became a writer. It stuck.

When I look back now, I wonder what else I might have learned about myself if I had let myself care. About anything. If I'd stopped resenting my peers who were having a better time and spent those years exploring my own interests. I wonder if I might have enjoyed acting, what I might have gained from playing intramural sports or singing in choir.

I did invest some, and in a turn of events that is perhaps only surprising to me, those things stuck. I was involved in activism and I took my writing class seriously. Both are now primary ways I identify myself. But I've made a conscious effort in my adulthood to show up for my life in a way I didn't then. To try new things and possibly be terrible at them. To get to know the people who are having a great time instead of roll my eyes underneath my invisibility cloak. To always be open to new interests, new ideas and all that a year in my life might bring me.

All that to say, high school might suck. Or junior high. Or your first year out of school. But if you ever find yourself in a space that doesn't feel inviting and you have to stay awhile, I really hope you allow yourself to make those years meaningful to you. I hope you never stop exploring yourself, your interests and what might bring you joy. This is all temporary, baby girl. Make the most of it.

On break-ups.

My first major break-up was with my high school sweetheart. I honestly thought I was going to die. Having been fully convinced that he was "the one" I would be with forever, I felt lost, confused and beyond repair.

We had a beautiful story. He used to walk me home from school in junior high. Brought flowers to my mom on Mother's Day. Always had a romantic, thoughtful surprise up his sleeve for Valentine's Day. He had worked hard to get my attention in the beginning and when we finally got together, I just "knew" this was "it."

He broke up with me because he had graduated from high school and I was still there. He wanted to explore new things and new people and that meant leaving me behind. In hindsight, these reasons all made sense. And actually weren't even that personal. He didn't hate me, didn't say terrible things about who I was, he just wanted to move on.

And yet I heard his thoughtful words about what he wanted for his own life and took them to mean I wasn't worthy of him. I believed I would never have another relationship like this. That if he wouldn't take me back I'd be doomed to be alone forever. A prospect that at the time seemed like actual hell. It felt like he took a part of me I would never get back. I was lonesome and sad and inconsolable. I cried nonstop for days only to continue to fall into fits of tears over this loss for many years.

I dated other people, but none who were as kind to me as he had been. Instead of continuing to search for someone who treated me well or (heaven forbid) enjoy getting to know my single self, I chose instead to look back only on our best times together. The fantasy of our "perfect" relationship popped into my head whenever I found myself alone. I obsessed over him in a way I can't say was becoming of me.

I reached out to him to try to make him change his mind. I want to say this was by inviting him to lunch and having a very grown-up conversation about our potential future together. But really this was by way of an embarrassing amount of text messages. If I'm being completely honest, it also involved hanging around outside his apartment on a couple of occasions, hoping to pull off "running into him" casually. I thought if I did the perfect combination of things to improve myself and keep showing up in his life that I could "right" the "wrong" of our relationship ending.

It worked. The relationship continued. But not in the way I had hoped. We spent time together. Time I put much more emotional stock in than it warranted. Time I was sure meant we would finally live our "happily ever after." Time I would spend copious hours dissecting after the fact. Analyzing every word, every glance, every last thing.

I know it sounds ridiculous. But it felt like my only option at the time. I thought if I kept trying harder I would finally win back the love I so desperately wanted to believe was mine all along.

We never did get back together. I learned a few lessons the hardest possible way, through tears and rage and primarily self-inflicted suffering. These may well be things you have to learn yourself as well.

But here is what I know now:

When someone says they don't want to be with you, it's best to believe them. Sure, there are a million possibilities as to why someone would say such a thing, and some of them are not genuine. But it is not up to you to sort that out for them. His intentions were clear and I not only didn't believe them, I also didn't respect them. I could have potentially saved myself from a lot of pain by simply listening to the words he said and took them as his truth.

Life is full of possibilities. While losing my first love felt like the greatest tragedy anyone had ever endured, he was not my one great love. In fact, he wouldn't even be the one to bring about the most heart ache. It's hard to believe when you are hurting, but there is always more for you. Even when moving forward seems impossible. You will.

Trying to convince someone to love you is the worst. It brings about more pain than the loss itself. You are completely worthy of love, as is, every day. Anyone needing convincing of that doesn't belong in your life.

Some people come for seasons. I loved him completely. And yet I know now that we are two people who are not meant for one another. We are fundamentally different in ways that would never have worked long-term. But I don't regret our relationship. He taught me so much about who I was, who I could be and what I was made of. I'll never forget those sweet memories we shared. But they were meant for high school me. Then the season was up. The trick is to appreciate the season you are in while you have it.

Leaving gracefully matters. Mostly to you. Cry, scream, find ways to cope, but when someone asks you to leave— leave. If this will become their greatest mistake, they will figure that out on their own. Not because you are on their doorstep to remind them.

Being alone it's own gift. It didn't occur to me at 16 that getting to know myself was valuable or even preferable to being in a relationship. I wanted someone to validate me. To think I was beautiful, charming, smart and worthwhile. When really what I needed was to spend time and energy investing in myself, in my own life, and the only relationship I will always have—with myself.

In those first days when I couldn't stop sobbing, I remember my mother's face. She was so worried about me and felt so helpless as to what to do for me. I felt bad for her but so lost in my own discomfort I couldn't see straight. You and I may have a similar moment one day. I just want you to know I will always listen, and that I do know how hard this is.

This stuff is hard. It's intimacy and loss and brings up every uncomfortable feeling you have in yourself about who you are. The truth is, my first love did take a piece of me that would never be returned. But the amazing thing about the heart is that it just keeps repairing itself. It keeps growing bigger in size. After losing someone you love, you may never be the same. But so long as your relationship with yourself expands, so my darling will you.

On driving.

Operate as though you are the most precious cargo there ever was, you are. Buckle up. Be sober. Call me if you aren't. Pay attention. I love you.

On intimate friendship.

Intimacy is a precious thing. For me it is sharing myself completely with another and trusting that they will love me anyway. Intimacy can be physical, but I think of it as more an emotional thing that has optional physical components.

I have many intimate friendships. Women with whom I feel no fear. I know I can show up exactly as I am, I can say what's on my heart. Women who will celebrate with me and hold space for me to completely fall apart. Who will listen and encourage and dance and rage with me—but always hold me accountable to what is mine to work through. With love, always with love. Women for whom I do the same.

It has always been these relationships that have pulled me out of the depths of myself when I get lost. It is to them I have leaned for support and gathered strength in my darkest hours. I cannot imagine my life without them.

I don't believe it's fair for any one relationship to be our "everything." That romantic or platonic, relationships require room to breathe, room for human error, room to not be the "other half" of anything, as we are all seeking to find ourselves to be whole.

I hope you find these relationships and cherish them with an open hand. With room for air and space enough for each of you to grow. Seek intimate friendships with people who are as prepared to support you when you are up as when you are down. It's easier to find folks who will revel in your darkness than who can withstand your light. And though it is perhaps the hardest kind of loss, let those go who cannot do both.

On what others think of you.

When I started sharing my writing publically, I took a lot of hard knocks to my self-worth. In my experience, women are more likely to be bashed for their appearance or ability to partner than for their actual work. My content has rarely been picked apart favoring instead to focus commentary on my looks or the assertion that "No man will ever want me."

The names I have been called since I began sharing of myself in this way have become some of the best gifts I have ever received. My skin is thick. My head is clear. I realize now that I cannot possibly do anything of value and expect only praise. And, over time, I have come to not take the praise personally either—seeing all of the commentary both as an opportunity for my own development and a reflection of the sender.

"How you feel about me is between you and your self-esteem." This is one of my favorite quotes of all time and I have no idea whom to attribute it. I heard a guy at a conference once say it and Google has failed me in my many attempts to decipher its origin.

I loved it then but it would be many years before I could actually live that way. To honestly believe that the way others felt about me said more about their relationship with themselves than it did me. But there are a couple of important notes to make about this. It's not merely an invitation to not be accountable.

The first is that this also applies to how you feel about others. Whenever someone brings about jealousy in you, that is also work required of you. Jealousy is an indicator of insecurity. It can also be a powerful indicator of what you want for yourself. Whether that is a positive moment of growth on your part or a nasty expression of your demons is up to you.

When someone says something critical about me, I don't simply chalk that up to being his or her problem.

I hold on to it for a moment. Ask myself if there is anything there that is true. Is any of this mine? Are they right? Is this something I am insecure about? Do I have work to do? We all have so much work to do.

The bottom line is that we cannot control others. We cannot control their perceptions of us. We cannot control what they think or say about us. Trying to do so is a full-time job and one you will always fail.

The best thing we can do for ourselves is to always be willing to show up to do our own work. To let go of the notion that everyone will agree with or like us. Instead focusing on making sure we are living in alignment with our own values.

Your perception of yourself is the one you walk around in every day. Be willing to look at it, grow in it, work through pieces you've picked up along the way that no longer serve you. And carefully hold others' words for consideration for your own development, but not at the expense of who you are.

Real power comes from your own sense of self. The more you look there, the more sturdy your own foundation becomes. And from the rock of your own creation, hurtful words begin to draw out compassion instead of anger. Peace instead of fight. Introspection instead of a sense of failure. This is hard work, baby girl, but it will ground you in your own feet like nothing else. I hope you show up to do it.

On pregnancy and motherhood.

Should you choose to conceive a baby, pregnancy is quite a miracle. I found myself amazed at all I didn't know I would experience. From the hormonal changes that created a roller coaster of emotions I felt simply along the ride for, to all of the daily changes in my physical body, to say I was unprepared is an understatement.

I remember feeling like this was so miraculous, and though pregnancy was nowhere near a new "phenomenon," it felt like this was the first time this had ever been done. There was a child in my body?! Growing inside me?! Kicking and napping and doing baby things?

As soon as I started to show, I also was shocked to find how much commentary my state seemed to require from relative strangers. People I'd never seen before would walk up and touch me in a way I couldn't imagine doing to someone else. And then come the questions which decidedly felt much more like judgements or opportunities to make speeches than actual curiosity.

Will you breastfeed? Are you going back to work or will you stay home with the baby? Cloth diapers or disposables? Each innocent seeming inquiry would launch the questioner into a diatribe about what was "best." Or worse, the dire implications of what happens if I make the "wrong" decision. "Here are a slew of ways you are already ruining your child, good luck!"

Having been a social worker for many years I have been privy to many different styles of parenting. I feel very certain that the following parameters make for a parent who is doing a "good job."

Loving their child to the best of their ability.

Making thoughtful choices with their child in mind.

I believe that looks different for everyone. Starting from the very beginning. I also think that this "Mommy wars" thing, where women feel pit against one another in all of their choices surrounding parenting has less to do with judgement and more to do with insecurity. I have yet to meet a parent who didn't worry she was getting something about it horribly wrong. Who didn't lose sleep at night sometimes wondering if she had failed her child that day.

So here are a few objective things about my own pregnancy that I wish I had known.

My body changed, possibly forever, and that is a beautiful thing. There is no reason to try to get a "pre-baby" body back because there is also no getting your "pre-baby" life back. It's all different. It's all beautiful. It's worthy of embracing.

My feet swole so big I couldn't wear any shoes but your daddy's athletic sandals. Everything felt big and swollen and confusing in that on a daily basis I was unsure of how much space I took up.

I didn't love everything about being pregnant and that's okay. Some parts I found magical and some parts (on-going morning sickness) were not fun at all. I don't think your experience can be "wrong."

I pooped on the table during delivery. Apparently that is normal. Everyone in the room lied to me about it. I didn't love that. I just feel like this is something you should know about. I'm continuously floored that while so many women have had babies, so few of the details are spoken of. I've often thought if men had babies their birth stories would be engraved on plaques, hung over mantles and discussed over whiskey after dinner. We however endure this incredible pain and bring life into the world and are never to speak of it again?

Labor was painful. But I walked away from that experience feeling unstoppable. Our bodies can do some amazing things. We can endure incredible pain and get up and walk after. That's amazing.

Breast milk comes out of multiple holes. Multiple holes! Meaning, you can squeeze a breast and the stuff comes flying out all different angles and directions. Why didn't I know that? Why was that not a part of my science classes at some point? Fascinating.

My "birth story" didn't go exactly as planned. The nurses thought my friend was my romantic partner and spent too much time focusing on their curiosity about our sexuality. I ended up taking drugs I hadn't planned on, but so late in the game that they weren't helpful anyway. My doctor wasn't available, so I endured the on-call doctor who's coaching felt more like I was playing little league football than giving birth. It just wasn't what I envisioned. And it was perfect just the same. It ended in you.

After going through this myself, I have more compassion for the strangers who couldn't help themselves to touch my belly. While those boundaries are questionable at best and deserve addressing however the "belly-haver" sees fit, I now understand the draw. I too see pregnant women and feel connected to them. I want some piece of that back, to touch a belly, to offer some advice. I refrain, because I remember how that felt. I only share advice if someone is seeking it, and then frame it all as openly as possible.

There is no way to get this stuff right. If you choose to conceive a baby you will likely feel all of these pressures and you will have to sort through them yourself. But the more secure you are in the notion that you are doing your best, the less it will bother you.

On marriage.

Your father and I were tired when we met. We were both in a place in our lives where we were exhausted by relationships that didn't work. While we were interested in one another, we were also a bit cynical. So we interviewed one another extensively.

We lived in different cities so we spoke on the phone at length. Sometimes all through the night. We asked questions about each other's childhood, if we wanted children and how we wanted to raise them. We asked about what had happened to cause our previous relationships to end and what we would do differently this time. We spoke about politics, religion, values, future plans, everything. We were seeking out "red flags," reasons not to proceed. And when we didn't find any we moved fast into a relationship that has now withstood ten years of hardship and triumphs.

But I don't think either of would say it has been easy. Neither of us is the same person we were ten years ago. We have evolved, some together and some independent of one another. We have sat down on many occasions for a sort of "state of the union," some of which we left feeling more defeated than having found resolve.

Having a roommate is hard. No one ever thinks the dirty dishes were their own creation. Laundry doesn't stop for anything. Negotiating bills, chores and all of the responsibilities that come with sharing a living space is challenging to say the least. Marriage includes all of those things and adds intimacy, sex, partnership, considering the impact of all of your choices on the other, commitment and all of the ways love presents itself in different seasons.

Ten years in I couldn't be prouder of how far we have come together. Of all we have set out to accomplish and supported one another through. No matter how far away from one another we travel, we always find our way back home. He smells like safety to me, like love, like where I belong. He is my person.

Before I began speaking honestly about my marriage with my closest married friends, I secretly worried I was failing at it completely. I thought that if we weren't feeling passionately in love at every turn it was doomed. I wondered if it was "normal" to ever have a doubt. I've come to believe it is.

Love doesn't feel like a choice. It hits you like a ton of bricks. Leaves you starry eyed and high for awhile. It waxes and wanes. It sometimes looks like unbridled passion and others like picking your socks up off the floor.

Marriage, however, is a choice. It's a commitment to homebase. It's showing up over and over and over to meet again the always evolving person you've chosen. It's family you get to pick.

Marriage doesn't complete you as I don't believe any person can. It can compliment you. It can mean always having that person who gives you the words you can't give yourself. For me, it means knowing someone always has my back and wants what is best for me. It's home. And yet each of us has to be complete in ourselves. We cannot create one another's happiness. We cannot hold each other accountable to what we must address in ourselves.

Part of why my marriage works for me is because I am not against divorce. I make no judgements about others' experiences, and honor that sometimes the most loving thing you can do for yourself or another is walk away. While I fully intend to grow old with your father, I feel even more love and commitment to us knowing that we are both choosing it. We aren't stuck here. The music didn't stop and we just ended up with this last option as in a giant game of musical chairs. We willingly choose to be us. Every day.

If you choose to get married, I hope you find someone who makes your life better by being in it. Who feels, smells, envelops you like home. And I want you to know that it doesn't have to look like anyone else's relationship to be wonderful. Nothing is only blue skies. Life isn't like that. It's a choice you keep making. And hopefully one that always comes back to a clear vision of why you began.

On conflict.

I have a simple rule of thumb for navigating conflict. For as long as I have used it, it has served me well. In relationships, and especially those that are important to me, I always aim to say the most true loving thing. That doesn't always come easy. But I have never regretted choosing the route of love.

Relationships can be hard. Feelings get hurt. Misunderstandings happen. All of those things are a part of life. The best way to handle them is directly and honestly, avoiding ongoing worry and drawing your own conclusions.

Saying the most true, loving thing is not blowing smoke. It isn't manipulation. It is searching for the kindest way to navigate the difficult waters of conflict. It requires you do the introspective work of owning what is yours and not "calling out" someone else on their shortcomings in an effort to belittle them. And it is seeking the most peaceful pathway to resolve.

I used to spend a lot of time picking apart others. Particularly those who didn't like me or with whom I was in conflict. I now know I did this primarily because I spent so much time picking apart myself. But I thought that analyzing someone else's behavior would make me feel better, make sense of it, perhaps even elevate me.

It doesn't.

The "best" result of spending your energy critically analyzing others is "getting to be right." Which is lonely at best and heart breaking at worst. When you attempt to build your own foundation on non-loving critical assessments of others, your own worth crumbles with it.

Aim to be direct. Settle disputes as they arise instead of spending all your energy making up stories about the situation that might not even be true. Seek to find your own fault in the matter. It's not about being wrong, it's about moving forward thoughtfully. Being open to growth. And choose the most loving true words to speak.

Sometimes the most loving true thing is silence. But I would rather be silent than to purposefully inflict pain.

On finding your voice.

An important part of my discovering who I was, was finding the strength to use my voice. To speak up for myself or others. To believe that what I had to say was of value to anyone. I still have to practice believing that today.

When I was younger I believed that much of the dismissal of my voice was to do with being young. I expected that as I got older people would put more stock into what I had to say. They would care more. I wouldn't be dismissed. I spent much of my youth feeling depreciated.

Having spent a lot of my junior and high school years depressed and not applying myself, I was worried I would get to college and find out I wasn't smart. But instead I did very well. I got involved with campus activist groups and, for the first time in my life, found value in myself outside of failing to be beautiful.

Some part of me was aware that I was "supposed" to be quiet and not rock the boat. So I was very thoughtful about how I went about being passionate. After work, class and studies I would pour myself over statistics. Memorizing facts so that when faced with difficult subject matter, ignorance or injustice, I could rattle off facts. This, I thought, is how I will ensure I am heard without being overbearing.

It didn't work.

My peers began rolling their eyes whenever I spoke in class. I was something of an outlier at the time and location. This wasn't particularly welcome.

So I began to be even more careful. Police my own "tone." Make sure I seemed friendly and smiled a lot. I started making little bargains with myself. I'll only speak on Wednesdays. Or only about certain topics. I spent a large amount of time and energy trying to find the perfect way to insert my voice, by narrowly defining how and where it belonged.

One day I was in a political science class when a male peer of mine didn't like what I had to say. Instead of address the subject matter, my words, he just began to attack me. He stood up in his chair, towered over me and raised his voice.

I remember feeling like I was having an out of body experience. My hands went up to my sides in disbelief. I looked around to see how others were responding, surely they are equally confused at this behavior.

Instead I saw people who were watching his tirade as though it was a noble act. From a group of students behind me I heard the words, "He's such a great leader. He should go into politics."

I was dismayed. For the first time in my life it was clear to me that my words and choice of expression were viewed very differently than my male peers.

I want to tell you that I stood up for myself. That I learned in that moment to stand for what I believe in no matter what. I want to tell a story where everyone cheered in the end. But what really happened next is that I began to drop out of my life. I went back to the numbing I had learned to do. I chose to miss out on another chapter that could have been great. I felt defeated and I decided to stay there.

The lesson I learned that day would serve me, but not until much later. When I started writing again and about things I am passionate. When I began fighting against the myths of perfection, the confines of beauty, for autonomy and self-governance for women. For you.

I don't know how this will change in your lifetime. And I don't have the answers as to how you will find your own voice. For me it has meant finding the things I care so much about, that no amount of opposition derails me. Since

I picked a pen up again, I have thought very little about how I might be received. If the classroom full of eyerolls will begin again. If I will be friendly enough or liked. What I do now matters so much more to me than any of those things.

For what it's worth, only speaking on Wednesdays didn't work. Neither memorizing statistics or carefully monitoring my tone. While it's a worthwhile to learn about effective communication styles, I've found zero ways to ensure my voice isn't met with some kind of scolding. So even when it quivers, I carry on.

So carry on, baby girl. When you feel your voice come all the way up from your feet you know you have no choice but to share it. When it matters most, the backlash is of little consequence. Your voice is mighty. It matters. It's yours.

On being your mother.

Becoming a mother is the scariest thing I've ever done. I remember thinking to myself that I could no longer hide from who I was, as you would shine it all right back at me.

I didn't plan you and yet you came right on time. Your very existence inspired in me a desire to look honestly at all of who I am, in order to be the kind of woman I wanted you to look up to. I have never felt more love or had to battle with more guilt. I struggle on a regular basis with the choices I make, if for a moment you are not at the center of each one. Which is not a feeling I expected, even having watched so many women before me struggle in that same way.

It's the hardest thing I've ever done. I'm not supposed to say that. It's the most wonderful thing I've ever done. The duality of that is hard to express.

It's an honor to be your mother.

I hope that where I've been and what I've learned can be of service to you. If only to understand better from where you came. I hope you always come back to me, even as growing might mean you sometimes push away. I love you to the moon and back and I always want what is best for you. I'm sure you will let me know when we disagree on what that is. And I sincerely hope I find the wisdom within me to listen.

Love, Mommy

31671738R00071

Made in the USA
Middletown, DE
07 May 2016